Christmas Trees

BY KATHRYN STEVENS

The Child's World®

Published by The Child's World®
1980 Lookout Drive • Mankato, MN 56003-1705
800-599-READ • www.childsworld.com

ACKNOWLEDGMENTS

The Child's World®: Mary Berendes, Publishing Director
The Design Lab: Design
Olivia Gregory: Editing
Pamela J. Mitsakos: Photo Research

Design elements ©: Kamenetskiy Konstantin/Shutterstock.com: ornaments
Photographs ©: Aleksei Potov/Shutterstock.com: 18-19; eans/Shutterstock.com: cover, 1 (tree); Dean Fikar/Shutterstock.com: 21; gkuna/Shutterstock.com: 15; irin-k/Shutterstock.com: 6-7; IZO/Shutterstock.com: 9; Lori Sparkia/Shutterstock.com: 16-17; Nejron/Dreamstime.com: 11; Sergey Furtaev/Shutterstock.com: 12-13; Steve Heap/Shutterstock.com: 5

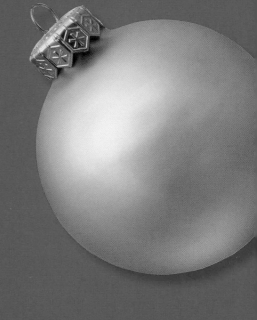

ISBN 9781631437427
LCCN 2014945400

Printed in the United States of America
Mankato, MN
November, 2014
PA02244

Table of Contents

It's a Christmas Tree!

You are sitting in your cozy living room and sipping hot chocolate. A big green tree stands in the corner of the room. It is covered with colorful decorations and lights. Wrapped gifts are piled around it. It's your very own Christmas tree!

People all around the world enjoy decorating Christmas trees. The trees are a fun way to spread holiday cheer.

Why Do We Decorate Trees for Christmas?

People have made trees a part of many holidays throughout history. People in Germany and Scandinavia brought trees inside their homes during the long winter. The trees reminded them of summer. People in Germany started using decorated trees in their Christmas celebrations. The idea spread to the United States and other countries.

Decorations are an important part of Christmas trees. They help give each tree its own special look.

7

What Kinds of Trees Make Good Christmas Trees?

The leaves of most trees change color and drop off in the fall. That is why Christmas trees are made from **evergreens**. Evergreens keep their green leaves all year long. Their long, thin leaves are called **needles**.

Evergreens can even keep their leaves during snowstorms. This makes them perfect for celebrating winter holidays!

9

What Are Artificial Trees?

Some people do not use real trees for Christmas. They use **artificial** trees instead. Some artificial trees look just like real ones. Others look very different. Some are even bright pink or shiny silver! Artificial trees can last for many years if they are stored the right way.

Where Do Christmas Trees Grow?

Some people cut wild trees to use for Christmas. One problem with using wild trees is that they do not always grow in nice shapes. Most people prefer to buy Christmas trees that are grown on special farms. Trees from tree farms usually have better shapes.

Choosing a Christmas tree is a fun holiday tradition for many families.

How Are Christmas Trees Grown?

Growing nice Christmas trees takes a long time. Baby trees called **seedlings** are planted in rows. They are planted far apart so they have room to grow. Growers start **shearing** the tips of the branches when the trees are about 2 feet (0.6 meters) tall. This gives them nice shapes.

Christmas tree farms can grow thousands of trees at once. This means there will be plenty for everyone at Christmastime.

How Are Christmas Trees Cut and Shipped?

Trees are cut down when they are big enough. Growers shake the cut trees to get rid of dead needles. Then the trees are wrapped in twine or plastic netting. Wrapping the trees is called **baling** them. Cut-off branches are also saved and sold. They are used for making Christmas **wreaths**.

Trees take up much less space when they are baled. This helps growers fit more trees on shipping trucks.

How Can You Choose a Nice Christmas Tree?

Choosing a tree is fun. Start by deciding how big a tree you need. Then think about what type to get. Should you get a tree with long needles or short needles? Make sure the tree is nice and fresh. The needles should be green and bendable.

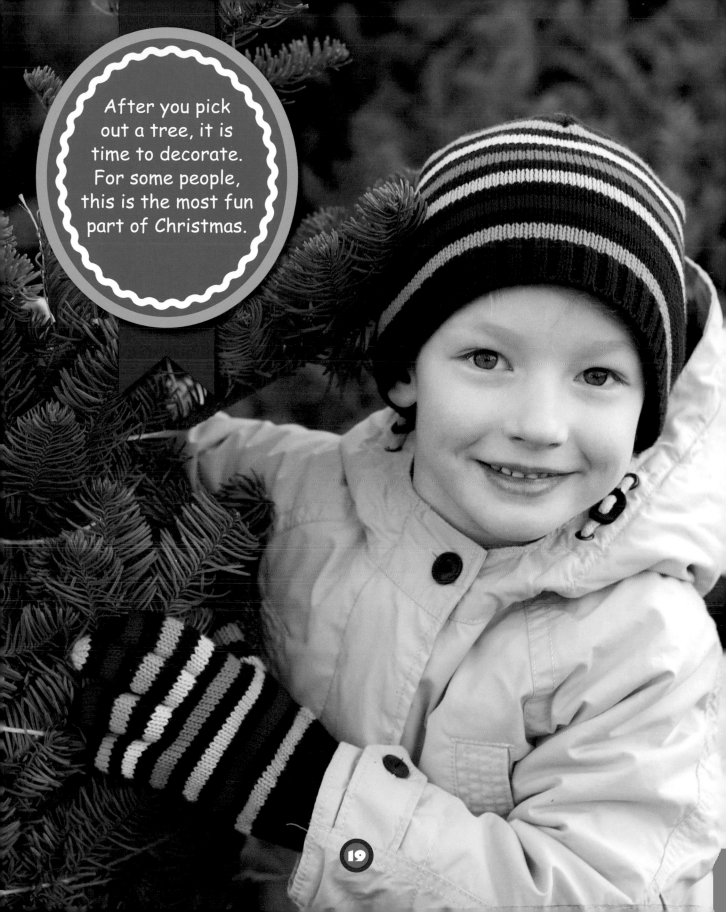

After you pick out a tree, it is time to decorate. For some people, this is the most fun part of Christmas.

Your Very Own Tree

Now you have chosen your tree. You brought it home and found the perfect spot for it. It is covered with decorations and pretty lights. It does not matter what kind of tree you picked. All Christmas trees carry the same message: "Have a Merry Christmas!"

The tree is decorated, and the presents are wrapped. It is time to enjoy the Christmas season.

GLOSSARY

artificial (ar-tih-FIH-shull) Something that is artificial is not real, even though it might look like the real thing. Artificial Christmas trees are made from plastic and metal.

baling (BAY-ling) Wrapping cut trees in twine or netting is called baling them. Christmas trees are baled to make them easier to handle and stack.

evergreens (EH-ver-greenz) Evergreens are trees with leaves that stay green all winter instead of changing color and falling off. Many kinds of evergreens are used for Christmas trees.

needles (NEE-dullz) The thin, pointy leaves of an evergreen tree are called needles. Different kinds of evergreens have different kinds of needles.

seedlings (SEED-lingz) Seedlings are very small trees. On Christmas tree farms, evergreen seedlings are planted in long, straight rows.

shearing (SHEER-ing) Shearing is cutting the ends off a tree's branches to give the tree a certain shape. Christmas tree growers use clippers or knives to shear the trees into pleasing shapes.

wreaths (REETHZ) Wreaths are round rings made from branches. Many people decorate their doors with Christmas wreaths.

BOOKS AND WEB SITES

BOOKS

Ingalls, Ann. *Christmas Traditions around the World.*
Mankato, MN: The Child's World, 2013.

Osbourne, Rick. *The Legend of the Christmas
Tree.* Grand Rapids, MI: Zonderkidz, 2001.

Purmell, Ann. *Christmas Tree Farm.* New
York: Holiday House Publishers, 2006.

Ray, Mary Lyn. *Christmas Farm.* Orlando, FL:
Harcourt Children's Books, 2008.

WEB SITES

Visit our Web site for lots of links about Christmas trees:
childsworld.com/links

*Note to Parents, Teachers, and Librarians: We routinely verify our Web links to make
sure they are safe, active sites—so encourage your readers to check them out!*

23

INDEX

ABOUT THE AUTHOR

Kathryn Stevens has authored and edited many books for young readers, including books on animals, countries, holidays, and instruments. A resident of La Crosse, Wisconsin, Kathryn is a lifelong pet lover and currently cares for a big, huggable pet-therapy dog named Fudge.